T0062318

fly in a beehive

*

Poems

Thato Tshukudu

Mwanaka Media and Publishing Pvt Ltd,
Chitungwiza Zimbabwe

*

Creativity, Wisdom and Beauty

Publisher:

Mmap

Mwanaka Media and Publishing Pvt Ltd

24 Svosve Road, Zengeza 1

Chitungwiza Zimbabwe

mwanaka@yahoo.com

https//mwanakamediaandpublishing.weebly.com

Distributed in and outside N. America by African Books Collective

orders@africanbookscollective.com

www.africanbookscollective.com

ISBN: 978-0-7974-8492-4

EAN: 9780797484924

Acknowledgements

I would like to express great gratitude to the many people who were part of my journey in writing poetry and compiling this book; to all those who offered support, offered comments and assisted in the proofreading, editing and design of this book. I would like to thank Hopewell Msimango and Bokgabane Thamaefor proofreading, analysing and editing my poems. I would also like to thank the following family members for the roles they played in supporting my journey in literature; Kgabo Tshukudu and Matsheko Madalane for financing my trip to *Mcgregor Poetry Festival* to attend the national poetry competition, in which I won first place, Boitumelo Moatshe for transportation from Paarl to Mcgregor and motivation to attend the event, Refiloe Tshukudu for encouraging and supporting my dream of publishing a book in my teenage years and Boipelo Tshukudu for the advice on the design and structure of the book. I also want to thank Tshepo Leie for all the interior graphics present inside the book. Above all, I would like to thank my mentor, book editor and publisher Tendai Mwanaka for the belief he has in my work and the motivation to be "a published, very young poet".

Table of Contents

Introduction

Dear reader,

First and foremost, I thank you for taking interest in embarking on this journey through myths, love, race, depression and secrets with me. I only wish that the poems in this book resonate with you on a more personal level and that they may offer some form of consolation or hope in your life.

Poetry has acted as a mode of healing, resurrection and fulfilment in my life. I compiled this anthology as an eighteen-year-old poet's dream of (finally) taking my passion to the next level. This is following four years of developmental growth in writing that I have taken the step to follow my most important dream of publishing a book of poetry which my peers will find very relevant in their daily pursuits in teenagehood.

I conjured up the title "Fly in a beehive" as an ambiguous metaphor for being the odd one out in a society that shackles free spirits. My poetry only serves to speak the truth I believe, and I am unapologetic about the notions which I may have broken to conceive this book. The second meaning of the title, which explains why I did not include an article to the title, is that we as individuals should not be afraid to fly into beehives (metaphor for any place outside of our comfort zones). One of the topics I raise in this book concerns race. It was not an easy task of overcoming the fear of judgment that would, and could, be catapulted onto me with the release of this book but, having chosen to be the voice of the silent; I have flown way outside my comfort zone in tackling issues I have less experience in.

Fly in a beehive is not a controversial conglomerate of views but merely the voice and heart of the people. It raises those issues which society deems taboo whilst oozing relatability in the process.

Fly in a beehive ranges from objective issues such as masculinity and racism to more personal issues such as love and loneliness. During its conception, I have come to understand the importance of having pre-set goals that scare the living daylights out of me. I am only eighteen and have already accomplished way more than what my sixteen-year-old self could have ever imagined. I hope that not only do the poems in this book speak light to the dark corners of your life, but the mere existence of this book encourages you to go out there, grab opportunity by its neck and suck out all that it must give.

Poem

Winning poems

These are the two poems I submitted to the Poetry in Mcgregor 2017 competition. The mandate was to submit a maximum of two poems that were in line with the topic "Poetry Over Poverty". "De Wet Street" won first place and "Redemption" took third in the national competition.

De wet street

It is 5 AM in De Wet Street
and the dying plants colour the garden with a somber tint of black,
the trees silhouette the sky like clouds of incense,
grass blades stand tall and proud carrying a pall of stale blood,
rusted fences not high enough to stop thieves from breaking in but
thin enough to filter the cold hymns sung in by the crow's laments,
street lights flicker like a dying star unable to emit anymore rays,
the dissipating tar road proudly reveals its cracks
and poverty sticks his nose out into the night
eagerly waiting for his prey

It is 6 AM in De Wet Street,
and as I stare out into the light skies
arid lips
bloodshot eyes
ribs prodding through my flesh and
my thin fingers firmly grasping onto my pen like a knife, I grimly
smile.
"I survived another night"

Redemption

Like water droplets plopping down from the rusted kitchen's faucet
to quench the thirst of the sink flange's arid throat
the ink in this pen silences the grumbling roars of my empty stomach
during hollow nights
this ink that scribbles stanzas of prayers
asking heaven to keep my malnourished brother alive till the next
dawn
and my mother's dying hope for employment still alive,
keeps my faith alive.

This ink that knits words together like fabric
ragged fabric draping my cold flesh against the harsh winter winds
sneaking in through the cracks of my broken bedroom window
translates poverty into mockery like
Poetry is not just words but medicine
that transforms chronic wounds and makes them mere acute wounds.

This ink that knows not of slavery but redemption
frees me from this life of rusted faucets and polluted water
frees me from this life of hunger and taunting whispers from the
vicious wind

This poetry is my fictitious wealth against
my actual poverty.

Masculinity and other myths

This chapter exposes a myth I believe should be discarded, masculinity.
"Let boys be boys" and "It is a man's world" are lies we groom our young generation to believe. No vile act should be justified merely because a man commits it and no woman should be subservient to a man's dominant demeanor. If a man wishes to turn on the waterworks, let him be. Gender should not drive superiority or emotions.

4

Silent victim, silent suspect

You sit peacefully
in the center
of a tornado

You lay restfully
in bed midst a
burning house

You stand unshaken
by the trembles
of a quake

As if You
do not notice
the destruction around You

As if You
are not unstable air,
a match stick &
a vibration.

Masculinity is a myth

Maybe I was just afraid of being heartbroken
so I amputated the branches of my limbs before they could bear
fruits wreathed in a bitter
taste of forever. Cut off these things like they
never carried your hips towards the skies to kiss shooting stars. Cut
them off like they never
folded into one to give birth to prayers that
made us possible. Cut them off to use the blood on the tips to
compose a symphony like, how
many falling heart pieces does it take to form
an orchestra? Sometimes I ask myself, did it hurt this much when I
nailed you on my heart hoping
you would stay there...forever?

{Untitled}

We raise our sons the same way we polish guns;
get them ready for a war they don't even know yet.

Beautiful beliefs

This Chapter introduces you to my views and beliefs on beauty and women.

 Feminine exculpation. Women are much stronger than men want to believe, and my belief is that if was a patriarchy-scorned society begin to commend women for their resilience throughout the ages, going forward, equality will start to smell more like reality than a myth. The chapter also touches on beauty. One can define beauty as being the component that makes people, objects or nature aesthetically pleasing but we seem to forget that beauty is far more internal than that. A nightingale needs to believe in its own voice before slipping a symphony out of its beak.

Survivor

I no longer call you a victim, just a survivor.
I call you survivor because you carry the war cry of your eternal
ancestors on the tip of your tongue
and a sharp breath in the abyssal depth of your open lungs so when
they attacked you let out a deafening roar like a charging army of
soldiers.
I no longer call you a victim, just a survivor.
I call you survivor because you carry the burden of the past on your
rear with no fear,
callous has formed but that is a small price to pay for a bloodline that
has handled the royal chalice.
I no longer call you a victim, just a survivor.
I call you survivor because of the way you walk like your entire form
was handcrafted from the bowels of pride.
Your impeccable strides leave deep depressions on the concrete
earth,
footprints deep as the impact your bloodline has left throughout the
generations.

I call you survivor because I also wish to survive the harshness of
time and come out of the storm looking less like a victim.

So much for "All" girl magic

At the end of this poem,
1 in 3 women will have suffered a concussion from a blow across the head by a man who
promised to "have and to hold" her in his safe arms. She will wake up in the aftermath of a
storm bruised. A repressed memory and a pack of antidepressants will convince her that
scars are a requisite for a "till death do us apart"
In a nearby neighbourhood,
1 in 5 women will have been raped. Her physical body battered to a pulp, she will attempt
to stagger to a nearby police station while onlookers whisper to their children to avoid
prostitution.
At the end of this stanza I will recall the day a buddy of mine catcalled a lady crossing the
street and I kept quiet or probably chuckled to the insensitivity of two boys seeing through
ahuman and classifying her as an object.

At the end of this poem,
The one I used to call my precious little baby cousin will have turned thirteen and
still pure as water.
From today onwards she will realize that the world is a dry and thirsty place
And these sharks all wish to drink at her oasis.

She will shrink her ocean into a puddle because sharks don't swim in shallow waters, right?
She will learn to recite the mantra that has kept her foremothers alive,
"Don't back talk the men that catcall you"
"Don't forget to smile when they ask for your numbers".

At the end of this poem,
My sister's cousin's friend is going to be buried under the silence of the period at the end of
this line.
Which is to say being female is to allow the hand that raised you to muffle your mouth and
steal your voice even when you know its first name and home address
Being female must be like wearing a crisp tailored suit on a Tuesday
Which is to say, there is no reason not to prepare the body for the casket when you are
female,
Prepare the soul for that which may be imminent on a Monday, or Wednesday or Sunday
because isn't death becoming a second shadow to my mother, sister, her best friend, my
cousin and her friend?

It is sad how this thanksgiving poem metamorphose into a eulogy
As if the only other magic trick women can perform is to stand tall and
Alive.

The pugilist reforms

Plough your gentle palm gracefully across her face and if she smiles
ain't it Amazing Grace?
ain't this Black magic without its blackness or all that is tragic?

See how you bloom sunflowers upon arid earth
and allow them to hold on a bit tighter to their roots till they too
believe that they can
blossom into the sun?

Can you see what happens when ore peels away from its skin and
your palm becomes the
mineral that nourishes her life?
Can you fathom this possibility?

Her beauty in 51 words

May I squeeze these twenty-four hours into
a second glance for two seconds spanned onto a
clean canvas? Your beauty breath-taking art brushstrokes
dipped into confetti rainbows colouring the palette.
Colour my palate like bubble-gum
trees taste like pepper
spearmint. Spare me
a minute longer
to indulge in
myown
elegance
.

Hello beautiful

she feared her insecurities
she said Insecurity was an itchy feeling under her skin
some nights too unbearable
she would claw the skin off her body
and sleep naked

she never knew what it felt like to live inside her own flesh
so when you called her beautiful
you saved her from herself

The appeal thesis

Moths:
Butterflies of the night eclipse my lantern's light
flap your beautiful wings with a thunderous might

    Ugly they say you are but
    i gape past the surface

Moths:
Butterflies of the night flare up for the light
their wings may span the heavens cloaked in rainbow patterns but
your
beauty lies within

{Untitled}

asteroids shed kilometers off their bodies before entering the
aerosphere
and sunflowers die after flowering.

sometimes we are the sacrifice to our new beginnings and
sometimes beauty be the birth of it.

Defence mechanism

She plucks Rosemary needles from the neck like guitar strings,
sings along to a song she knows all too familiar,
"He loves me, he loves me not"

She is the type to strangle the wine out of cranberries
and use the flesh to dress her wounds.
the type to sing Hail Mary through an eerie alley
as if to cloak the gloomy grey with a silky lace.

She is the type to watch Tom and Jerry after Buck's death in
Huckleberry.

She is the type to dress an excuse from the head down
when you see her emotions semi-nude.
the type to gracefully wipe the tears off her face
and call it yawning.

She is the type to grab the knife by the sharp end
and call it self-defence.
the type to recommend a holy prayer
when she herself knows not how to repent.

She is the type of girl that turns written poetry into scriptures;
she is a code, a hieroglyph, a cryptic note you must read twice
to realize that she is not impossible to love...
she just has a defence mechanism

Being black

This chapter touches on the hardships of being black.

Racism, slavery and wars are some of the few factors that have limited the black mind from reaching its full potential. In this chapter I unleash my frustrations on these factors, reminding the black man to hang on just a bit longer because his time for mental, physical and economical freedom and independence is yet to come.

Dinner at my friend's house

Josh invites me for dinner at his house
and the first thing I notice at the end of the table is an antiqued
crimson bowl shedding from
its coat.
No one talks of the bowl.
No one wants to touch the rusted bowl laying on the corner of the
satin lace covered dinner table.
No one wants to pour, sip, wash, rinse from the bowl.
We all know what is inside the bowl.
We all know that graveyards may hide the skeleton, but the epitaphs
engraved on the
tombstone is all the autopsy we need to recreate the dead.

I stare at Josh and back at the pigment of my forearm.
No one wants to talk about the bowl,
I also pretend like it's not there and
enjoy dinner.

Arson

My brother was cremated.
he is reborn as ash smoke eclipsing memories
his charcoal soul morphs into a face, a body and then a hand reaching
out from a purgatory
but these claws cannot seem to pull him back into the realm of the
breathing

My brother was cremated.
i think i heard a chuckle or a crackle, a distinct chortle followed by a
pop
he really had a thing for lollipops,
maybe if he didn't go to the shop that day
i wouldn't be writing this poem.

My brother was cremated.
his arid dust dresses the soil with a cloth of death.
the Southern swoops his weightless corpse onto nostrils, he smells
like a soulless breath.

My brother was cremated.
death is painted on air molecules which mommy inhales
he remains inside her lungs like a cancer she does not want to exhale

My brother was cremated.
i never managed to make it to his funeral,
i could not attend the final farewell of a ghost fused with the scents
of grief.

Mommy always warned us not to play with fire
because we would get burnt
but why didn't mommy tell the hooded man the same thing?

Oh look, i found the black ulnar nerve!

If people did not tame the wolf's mind, there would be no dog.
If people did not tame the human's mind, there would be no black
people.
It's funny how we smile when the sky is skin clear
and tremble in fear when she starts developing blackheads
like darkness is only a symbol for fear
and whiteness a motif for our security in this horror novel

Isn't it funny how black coffee is stronger without Cremora?
How dark soil is the most fertile?
How this melanin is offspring of the earth
yet we bleach... I mean believe that such pigmentation is a curse on
this white... I mean default flesh

Isn't it funny how we slave to taste the white man's money...I mean
honey?
Isn't it funny how we are BEEs striving to please self-ordained Kings
and Queens?

Isn't it funny how dark chocolate enhances the taste of white
chocolate
yet it's always on the bottom deck?

Isn't it funny how we wear white at weddings and black at funerals?
Isn't it funny how black is expected to wear black like a silky eulogy?

Isn't it funny how history is like a blank paper?
You only need a stroke of black blood… I mean ink on it for the
story to exist

Isn't it funny how this poem is not even about racism…I mean
slavery… I mean...
isn't it just funny?

Black boy cries wolf

Silly black boy cries wolf
silly black boy forgets he is no wolf
silly black boy is prey
praying for protection from the light
silly black boy forgets that black boys die in the light too
silly boy forgets that this skin ain't no longer safe in the hood too

He forgets that his pathetic roar calls out the Wolves from their
public dens
he forgets that his playground has turned into crosshairs for trigger-
happy animals
silly boy forgets how his brother's dried-up corpse still hangs on the
lips of a crooked judge with a tongue glistening bastard hope for
justice,
(Lips: a purgatory for black souls who were just
at the wrong place, at the wrong time.)
and how the previous "accident" left his neighbour's corpse flooding
the sidewalk in a blood bath for
two days

Silly black boy
forgot to tell mommy that he is going to the shop around the corner,
i don't blame him
he probably forgot that he is no longer the wolf; he is a puppy in the
wild

24

Silly black boy
thinks it is funny to make fun of the wolves
silly black boy cries wolf once
and his corpse gets crucified on corrupt lips
before it gets buried under hashtags,
but isn't that just the perfect metaphor?

To the white ladies who ask me, "do you work here?"

I am not sure what hurts most?
You, implying that the clothes I wore today, even after ravaging
through the entire wardrobe to find
what I assumed was swaggy, look like this store's uniform? Or

You, being able to see through this detergent-soaked flesh to
perfectly recognize my lineage even
after decades my great grandmother scrubbed slavery from her bitter
tongue to teach my
grandmother, who taught her daughter to teach her son the language
of equality and forgiveness?

I am not sure what hurts most?
Me, walking inside a store for a packet of sweets only to trip over a
mistake that landed me
somewhere in the 40s or 60s
amidst a conversation between some fifty-year-old white ladies
sipping on black tea
and I having to submit to their every instruction,
"Yes baas, I'm on it baas, may I take a break baas?" Or

You, being able to see through this white smile
your eyes landing somewhere
beneath this long sleeve hoodie, long denim pants and being able to
sniff out the melanin layered

26

deep under my model C English, suburban townhouse and city
school façade?

I am not sure what hurts most?
Me, responding with a chuckle? Or
you, expecting me to still point you towards the cleaning products
aisle
as if I haven't already been generationally stain-washed from
Apartheid

Dear white ladies, "No, I don't work here...my dad owns the store".

Letter love and loss

This chapter begins with a more heavy-hearted topic, love.
We all love. We all want to be loved. Being a poet makes this topic much more
interesting as it gives me the stage floor to hyperbolize and sentimentalize this
model, concept, feeling or whatever you wish to call it, from my own experience

This chapter also pokes on the wounds caused by love.Not all relationships
are letter-love type. Most times we fall head-over-heels in love (the correct term here
is "infatuated") with the wrong person and that leads us to discover what I call
painful passions; an alliterated expression for heartbreak. This chapter speaks for
itself.

Honey kisses at the beach

maple syrup supple slowly from spoon to lips
    golden touch turns tin lips into skin
molten flesh fire fireworks trips onto chin
disguise a ghostly grin; gin.

salty sweet sea waves swish
onto tongue shore seals shin
 on hind legs.
Drowning; the least of my worries.

Impossible possible love

I love you like bees and honey
this is to say,
Love is hard work.

I love you like midnight and the moon
this is to say,
even in my darkest you light up my world.

I love you like asphalt and tires
this is to say,
any journey is a destination when I'm with you

I love you like birds and chirping
this is to say,
your name is the only language I want to sing

I love you like the wind and trees
this is to say,
through the strongest gusts I'll still be standing here

I love you like sunsets and horizons
this is to say,
your eyes are the only proof I need to believe a heaven exists

I love you like today and tomorrow and the next day and the day
after
I love you like every day,

I love every day that has a shadow thought of you passing past the
canvas of my memory

I love the feeling I get when I say I love you
I love you like the three words are spirits;

I love you in time and space like
a heavenly body with a gravity enough to engulf the both of us in
your orbit
me, as a star or an asteroid, just floating in the aura of your
existence, in a limbo of I want you but can't touch you
like without you,
I am just another lung less breath
this is to stay,
this love right here
is the reason I breathe.

Deadly vows from a lonely widower

My tongue is a history lesson of all the memories we shared:
dates, times and locations all neatly organised on each taste bud

You have found shelter on my tongue
as a slave to hope

Too afraid to speak,
too afraid to let you escape

I spent an eternity with locked lips,
allowing myself to be choked by your longing for freedom.
You died on my hands and resurrected on my tongue and I'll
never ever let you leave me again.

i wish i'd said

If my mind is a morgue for the cold thoughts that died in veins,
then my heart is a casket of all the words that died in vain
and my passive face, a concrete plaque engraved with Rest in Peace
and my lips the infertile roses that could never spread pieces of me.

My hands, the spades that split grains of sand on the grave
now fold into one and ask for forgiveness
with two knees rooted in the ground as if the tears that flooded the
ground would breed a new
plant of resurrection

You never found out how I felt about you, so
when I recited your eulogy I had to be sure to start with; I am sorry.

pillow remorse

my poems are bones
stored in an ossuary
growing flesh
through rust.
you have a body
recreating itself under your pillow
and you don't even know it.

my poems are seeds
planted in a garden
growing limbs
through soil.
you have roses
blossoming under your pillow
and you don't even know it.

my poems are prayers
muffled under your clamorous thoughts
growing faith and blessings
through suicidal thoughts.
you have an antidote for the depression
silenced under the pressure of your pillow
and you don't even know it.

my poems are;
resurrection,
growth,

healing,
all under your pillow
and you don't even know it.

Le Chatelier effect

I loved you until all that was left was hate
turned a garden of roses into a skeleton church
whispers from dead leaves heave the scents of distrust,
how did we get from passionate touch to scattered dust?

Dear reckless red riding hood prancing joyfully on neckless daisies
teach me how to love again or at least...

how to move on.

Love like mosQUITo

Your love was like a mosquito kiss;
I only felt it when you left.

poets bleed too

she asked if poets bleed too
and i promptly responded, you are my rose
and her rose gold petal smile blossomed into a kaleidoscope of
happiness
and i just stood there wondering if she knows...
i meant the stem

The moon killed the sun

I watch as he brims the horizon with my eyes gleaming crimson
flames ofastar laid to rest in a coffin of silhouetted buildings
like the clouds with their ghost arms could not hold up such
a beautiful masterpiece

Iwatch as the grass blades lament the death of Ra
with arms waving hysterically towards his birthplace, the sky, hoping
for a sign that promises resurrection

Soil begins to deteriorate to give birth to a dirge the night crawlers
sing on their nightshifts,
Vampire trees stained with Ra's blood of wine passionately siphon his
blood like a gulag baby gulping down breast milk,
light rays hang onto invisible stars in the sky like steel arms sheltering
a beloved one
holding tight
holding onto the last piece of memory close to home

Losing his grip, I watch as his living corpse sinks into the dead earth
and a teardrop from his lover's companion star accompanies his body
like rose petals falling onto a casket

He dies when his lover arrives to steal his place in the sky and
she colours the night with purity as if she is not a murderer

But isn't that what love is about?
Doesn't it start killing you when it arrives but
you only start feeling like a corpse when it leaves?

i hate loving you

i
caught
your teardrops
with malnourished hands
and my thirst was quenched;
i only seem to find peace when
the thing you cherish most is
trapped between my
clenched
fists.

Why all cheaters are lemons

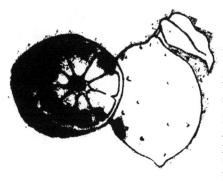

from far it appears orange.
its lips taste sweetly sour.
and though its truth tastes
foreign to your tongue,
you preserve it
believing that
Lemons
taste better
when
Lemonade.

Death and depression

This chapter resonates with me the most, touching on the essence of death through loneliness, suicide and addiction.
I may have not endured the burdens of depression myself but the real reason why I started writing poetry four years ago (2013) was to use it as a mode of cleansing. Being a silent soul, I have found it difficult to express myself emotionally through other people therefore I learned to suffer alone, allowing insecurity's louses to eat me up inside. I have met people in my life who have suffered the whips of depressions and still live to tell their stories. I write about suicide and depression to let those who are still victims of this atrocity to still have hope.
This chapter walks you through the dark parts of my life. Tread carefully.

On the train back to Hatfield a poet pretends to heal a stranger

"so how many
memories are you going to try on tonight?"
"do those scars have meaning?"
"i think you have a holding-onto-the-past problem "
"do you also hold onto things that are no longer tangible"
"do you have a name for your depression?"
"you know you can talk to me, right?
let me get your numbers"

the poet gets off the train and heads home to write a poem on
depression.
how beautiful it is to be a poet.
to be both hunter and coroner,
to go out into the wild,
come back with a soul,
spread it across the steel table
and perform an autopsy on it.

people are only as dead as a poet wants them to be
and poems are only as great as the dead want them to be.

Prayer from loneliness

I filter this prayer of despair between the cage bars of my clenched
fists.
This prayer seeps out and fountains down my carpals like blood in
veins escapes
through my hands, like freedom:

I am a prison or a cell within a prison.
Isolation;
I am confined in the cell or a coffin
like a corpse craving for the touch of a stretched light ray or
an incandescent glint of hope from the heavens to
keep me company or to share this life sentence with me for
an eternity
until this prayer evaporates into a message,
a light ray or a friend

To the person who walked inside my room while i was sleeping and asked

'Why do you love sleeping alone?'
i don't.
Insecurity just likes the right side of the bed more,
so i give him enough space to sleep.

Some days

Some days, the lilies and lilacs pour perfumes of antidepressants into the atmosphere, and I plant my nose in their leaves and hallucinate from their aromas.
Some days the garden is fumigated with a smell of thirst, from the xylem veins pumping erosion through their bodies, I smell death.
Some days I see soil, her body that brings life protruding from her like birth.
Some days I see tar, her body in a coffin stumped on by jovial juveniles dancing on the tombstones of their ancestor's graves.
Some days the world comforts me in the cave of her taste buds.
Some days she spits me out onto the cold sidewalk like chewing gum.
Some days I stare at the stainless-steel kitchen knife, wondering how many bottles of red wine are needed to cloak this brown flesh with a red garment.
Some days I don't wonder…
Some days I cleanse the sins of my body with a baptismal tear drop.
Some days the tears are acid. Racing down my face on to my hands like a dragon's teardrop, I burn.
I am my own pollution.

Some days I look at the clouds, morphing into wonderful shapes.
Some days the clouds are smoke, I choke.
Some nights, prayer is a foreign tongue I was once eloquent in.
Some nights she is a thesaurus who comforts me in her similar experiences.
Some nights Sadness and I sleep.
Most nights he prefers bedtime stories.

Some nights I walk up to my mother's door, cripple my fingers into a
fist and yearn to knock,
wait for her to stand midst the doorframe with sleepy eyes to comfort
me with a tired prayer.
Some nights I just stay in bed and just assume that everything will be
fine.

Depression, nights and suicide

You quench your thirst with quatrains
in the night when it rains
the pain slowly fades,
like a tear drop scurrying down your face or
a rain droplet scurrying down to the window pane

Forming a vein of tales,
warping time and space,
night seeking for sun streaking
rays for the dawn of day.
You lay startled and dazed as

your soul begins to vigorously
phase
through the physical form,
yourcage.
The physical pain slowly feints
and the spiritual weight causes
your soul to faint

Afraid, you impatiently wait for day to wake
before the hail of rain of pain blows you away
aiding you aimlessly astray to a deadly fate.
You die in vain.

When day finally approaches your
way
with its beaming rays and gait,
you dawn a mask on your face and
erase the stains of pain as

you gaze in a broken mirror.
Gaze at the reflection of a
repentant sinner.
I never knew your heart ached
so much on the inner. You
carried a burden of lies all
throughout the day till dinner

skipped dinner, I noticed that you are getting thinner and even lied,
told me it was a fever.
You tried taking your life and failed, I guess it was beginners luck.
I pray your pessimism withers
so you may live on to witness the next winter

Rose theory

Roses grow when they cry
and wilt when they die.
There is growth in pain
and pain in death.

Paper cuts

Paper cut
a slit on my heart
staples hug
my heart into one

Paper cut
guillotine on a dove
pain can chop your soul into half

Paper cut
i sleep around one
the stars and skies
know this is no farce

Paper cut
a scar on my arm
like an engraved tattoo,
Depression is art.

Five senses for the atheist

Pitter patter
a summer sprinkle
drizzles onto my rusted
palms and breaks my bones:

> My body
> a brittle shelter
> built on sacred ground
> this temple worships no god.

Pitter patter
a summer sprinkle
evaporates onto my nose
petrichor scents are dead prayers:

> My body
> is kept upright
> by a clotted prayer
> this temple cracks as it stands.

Pitter patter
a summer sprinkle
such salty delight
carries drudgery to my taste buds:

> My body
> has lost its
> voice. It no longer
> tastes the fruity flavours of prayer.

Pitter patter
A summer sprinkle
lands on my eye
I do not bother blinking:

fly in a beehive

My body
used to pray to
whatit could not see.
Do the blind see heaven?

The day my friend lost his stutter

I had a friend who used to stutter.
With a cluttered vocabulary and
jaws that fluttered every time he uttered a word
he was never the sociable brother within the brethren.

I had a friend who used to stutter.
Though his stutter gave conversations a bit of colour,
it became tougher to decipher his stutters as we grew older
he was never the expressive brother within the brethren.

I had a friend who used to stutter.
He lost his mother one summer
and because his father was not a lover
he had to act tougher than he was because his dad always said,
"Son, you ain't never heard of a crying trucker".

I had a friend who used to stutter.
It was not until that midsummer I discovered that my friend suffered
from sadness,
after supper I caught him with a wire cutter stroking his upper neck.
He fought back the tears as he spluttered a response,
"atatat least you have aveave a mother therther".

I had a friend who used to stutter.
He was never the expressive brother within the brethren.
It took him two summers to cure his stutter…
his father was the crying trucker at the funeral.

Magic tricks for attention

The audience is speechless.
I grab an onion with both hands and slowly
peel away its flesh but the aromas leave me still-faced.
I do not cry.
It's a magic trick.

The audience is speechless.
I soak my body in a pool of acid and swim swiftly along
its lips but the acid expires on my skin.
I do not burn.
It's a magic trick.

The audience is speechless.
I rest my body on a bed of needles
but the tips kiss my back like acupuncture.
I do not sting.
It's a magic trick.

The audience is speechless.
I bash my temple against a wooden wall.
I have learnt to speak destruction using parts of myself.
I do not hurt.
It's a magic trick.

The audience is speechless.
I wave a razor blade in the air, but it slips
and cuts my wrist.
The audience leaps to their feet and cheer in amazement but...

I do not tell them it's
not a magic trick.

family fiends

This chapter is probably my most personal one.
No family is a perfect family. I titled this chapter "family fiends" because it refers to those generational curses that plague our families: alcoholism, infidelity or domestic violence. As you walk through this cave remember that ghosts have arms too.

Lonely Spirit

Every night I console my soul with a bottle of hope.
Like the only reason why my lips caress the brim of this premium
blend is to allow its holy
water to baptise the tongue which was born from sin.
I repent with this bottle of hope kneeling on my flat breast, tears
strolling quietly down my
cheeks as if they had not precipitated from a deadly storm.
I marvel at the tails of veins bulging from my right hand yearning to
make indefinite
connection with what I call hope,
I stare in awe at the resistance, as if in a tug-of-war with good and
evil as the brim
approaches my lips.
How can hope taste so good and yet be so evil?

When you are stuck between loneliness
and a thousand voices yelling out your sins
binging on pints of hope seems like an easy way to silence the
screams,
you learn to scavenge for peace in the serenity of turmoil because
loneliness is the better fiend.

Our Father

My father,
hallowed is the name of a hypocrite hiding behind piousness.
Beguile us with a violet smile and pseudoscience but
this virus is the one thing I will not inherit from you.

My father,
thy may not see the kingdom as it comes
but at least thy haveth a net income.

My father,
who art in earthly havens
heaven painted me as a replica of you;
i guess this portrait has no value.

My father,
you indulged in earthly pleasures
and corrupted your own soul.
We now tuck your ghosts to sleep in the P[s]alms of this bible,
allow them to be angels in the daylight
because in my family, the devil is better accepted as Lucifer.

My father,
i am glad you could provide us with daily bread
but sometimes love is more filling than butter spread.

My father,
you were lead into temptation
and fed yourself into evil for that

i prayi get delivered through this primeval damnation,
Amen.

When my father asked me...

What do you want to be when you grow up?
And I answered "Astronaut"
What I actually meant was
"Anything but you"

Like silhouettes

Silhouettes: the ever-present not so real people.
Always there
but not even there.
That is what it is like to have a father
who was there
but not even there; a silhouette.

When your father is a silhouette
you learn to embrace memories tightly until you suck the past out
their bones

When your father is a silhouette
your mother masters the art of Sciography,
carefully constructing silhouettes that portray your father as a work
of art,
leaving you to fill in the featureless voids of the skeleton

When your father is a silhouette
you learn that not all shadows belong to bodies
nor all bodies belong to their silhouettes

When your father is a silhouette
you ravage through the remnants of his footprints and shadow
keeping every bit and piece of his existence tucked under your pillow
hoping that when you wake up
the tooth fairy will have swapped the silhouette for the real thing

Recursion

Look how the boy falls off the family tree,
but still breathes on impact.
How he merges with the ground
to be buried alongside ancestors he has been escaping his life.
See how the boy phantom rises from the grave
And crawls up the tree to escape his roots
reaches the shoot
and again, dives off...splat.
isolated his breath is that it yearns escapism.

If the boy doesn't fall far from the tree
does he still inherit his father's scars and broken bones?
Or does he keep on trying until he cannot no more.

Printed in the United States
By Bookmasters